ONLINE MARKETING FOR YOUR LOCAL BUSINESS

Your guide to finding new customers, retaining old ones, cutting your marketing costs, and increasing revenue by using the Internet to sell to people in your town.

Paul D. Stevens

Bootstrap Books Publishing

2011

Paul Stevens
Visit my website at www.bootstraplocalmarketing.com or contact me:
paul@bootstraplocalmarketing.com

Printed in the United States of America
First Printing: December 2011
For information about this title, contact the publisher:

Bootstrap Books Publishing
RR #1
41 Beamish Road
Hastings, Ontario
K0L 1Y0

publisher@bootstrapbookspublishing.com

Stevens, Paul

Online Marketing for Your Local Business: Your Guide to Finding New Customers, Retaining Old Ones, Cutting Your Marketing Costs, and Increasing Revenue by Using The Internet to Sell to People in Your Town./Paul Stevens – 1st Ed.

1. Local Marketing 2. Internet Marketing 3. Small Business
4. Self-Help/Business

Printed in the United States of America

10 9 8 7 6 5 4 3 2 1   11 12 13

DEDICATION

Lynn, Nathan, Shannon, Trevor, Kate, Gordon, and Dad. My inner circle.

Paul Stevens

CONTENTS

The time has come when advertising has in some hands reached the status of a science.

—Claude C. Hopkins, 1923

ACKNOWLEDGEMENTS

Nobody does it all on their own. We all have debts to those who went before, helped us along, cheered from the sidelines, and even to those who got in our way.

My family has been my inspiration. They never doubted my ability, though there were questions about whether I would ever actually get around to it—legitimate questions, too, since there are always more ideas coming down the track to distract and lead astray. I am living proof of the "shiny object syndrome." Thank God I'm not a fish.

I would also like to thank all those friends and acquaintances who listened, asked, discussed, and added to my personal body of experience and knowledge.

I would like to acknowledge my deceased wife, Suzanne, who had faith in me, loved me, and always believed I would eventually get published. Thank you Sue, I hope you can hear me.

In particular I would like to thank my daughter, Shannon, and her husband, Gord, who actually published a book and thereby prompted me to finally publish this one. I would like to thank my son, Trevor, a writing machine of the first order, who assisted Gord and Shannon. And, perhaps most important of all, I would like to thank Lynn, my wife, who puts up with my quirks, flights of fancy, and procrastination. Thank you for understanding Lynn.

1 THINGS ARE DIFFERENT NOW

The explosive growth of the Internet and consumers' acceptance of it has led to a fundamental shift in how businesses must keep in touch with their potential customers and clients. Facebook, Local Search, Twitter, smart phones, and the flood of online information provide today's consumers with access to more and faster means of finding what they want, where they want, and at prices they want than ever before.

This year there are 17 states in the US where they don't automatically deliver the telephone white pages anymore. According to AT&T, in places where people have a choice, only two percent of customers asked for a print copy.

Think about how this impacts the Yellow Pages. Publishers get to charge more for wider circulation. They absolutely *want* to see mandatory delivery. In fact, in San Francisco, where people were given a choice whether to receive the Yellow Pages or not, the Yellow Pages Association sued the city. The Association was afraid of what might happen to their business if people were allowed to opt out of receiving the directory. What does that tell you about consumer behaviour? If you are relying on the Yellow Pages for the bulk of your business, you can expect things to get worse than they are today.

If you depend on TV, newspaper, or radio advertising to draw in customers, take a look at the following trends among the 18–29 and 30–49 year-old age groups in the chart on the next page. I think you will find it illuminating.

TV, newspaper, and radio are all falling as news sources, across all ages from 18 to 49. Newspaper decline is the greatest in the 30–49 year-old group. What does that tell you about your advertising dollar use in this medium?

And what is the only medium trending upward? You guessed it. Now here's the key question: As your marketing dollar effectiveness has been falling in the old media, have you been spending money on the new?

Sources for News, According to Consumers, By Age							
	2004	2005	2006	2007	2008	2009	2010
18–29							
TV	66%	62%	62%	68%	59%	56%	52%
Internet	38%	25%	32%	34%	59%	56%	65%
Newspaper	30%	29%	29%	23%	28%	25%	21%
Radio	25%	21%	16%	13%	18%	17%	15%
30–49							
TV	74%	70%	68%	71%	68%	67%	63%
Internet	26%	26%	33%	32%	47%	42%	48%
Newspaper	42%	30%	31%	26%	28%	25%	22%
Radio	23%	17%	16%	15%	19%	20%	19%

Source: Pew Research Center for People and Press. "Internet Gains on Television as Public's Main News Source," January 4, 2011

Or look at the following report from the spring of 2011:

"Circulation fell at most of the largest US newspapers compared with a year ago, despite new rules that give publishers more flexibility to boost their totals." *The Associated Press, Tuesday, May 3, 2011*

Consumers are spending more and more of their time online, whether they are sitting in front of a computer, using their smart phones, or watching Internet feeds on their TVs.

How are you going to reach them? That's what this guide is about.

The Internet has opened up a world of possibility that you may only vaguely be aware of. It's a world beyond the past tried-and-true methods of newspapers, radio, Yellow Pages, radio, and TV. You now can provide consumers with critical purchasing information through local search optimization, websites, blogs, auto responders, social media like Facebook and Twitter, bookmarking sites, podcasts, and video through distribution outlets like YouTube. Consumers can customize their exposure to commercial messages through their personalized news alerts, text messaging, RSS feeds (a format for delivering rapidly changing web feed content), review sites, and friends' "likes."

It doesn't take a genius to figure all this out, but you do have to be aware of it. And whether you do the work yourself or have someone else do it for you, you need to have a strategy and to make some decisions.

This will require some effort. Either you, one of your family members, one of your staff, or a third party will have to do some writing, take some pictures, do a little taking, and maybe shoot some video. The good news is that all of this will probably cost less money than you are spending on marketing right now. And you don't have to switch everything all at once. You can take some time to find your way around, to figure out what you are comfortable doing yourself and what you might want to have someone else do.

Regardless, in this book I am going to show you how to get started. We will talk about what to do, why to do it, how to do it, and what tools you need.

So, without wasting any time on more talk, let's jump right into it.

Bonus:

If you would like to download video segments that demonstrate some of the skills described in this book, go to bootstaplocalmarketing.com.

There I have screen captures of me walking you through keyword analysis, Google Places listings, directory searches and web page analysis. All you have to do is let me know where you got your copy of the book and I will send you the link.

Paul Stevens

2 What Are Your Customers Looking For? Or, Keywords for Dummies

You may have incredible products or services. They could be sterling quality, competitively priced, and one hundred percent guaranteed—but if you call them *whizbangs* and your customers are looking *whatchamacallits*, you are going to have problems.

It is absolutely key to Internet marketing to know the search terms that will be used., and there is no way around it! You need to do some research before you do anything else.

Let me give a simple example from real life, using Google, Google Maps, and the Google Keyword Tool. I was talking to a local artist who sold pottery from her home. She had an attractive website and also had some space in a storefront in town. She wanted to generate more customers using her website. So I suggested we take a look at what a Google Maps search would bring up. Google Maps is the "go-to" vehicle to find out where any service or product is in your local area.

A search for "potters near Peterborough Ontario" turned up nothing but Google Maps asking whether I meant a magician with the last name of Potter, located near Port Hope. A search for "pottery near Peterborough Ontario" pointed to a selection of potters' studios and locations selling pottery. Much better.

Now it was time to turn to the Google Keywords Tool. Using the same phrases as above, the Keyword Tool showed that the phrase "peterborough pottery" generated just over 90 searches a month—whereas "peterborough potter" showed no results!

You might think that that was enough information, but there are some additional important points to consider. The Google Keyword Tool doesn't show results for less than 10 searches a month. And another interesting result was that the number of local searches for the generic term "pottery" numbered about 450,000; the number of searches for "clay potter" was 8,100—in other words, about two percent of the more popular term. We know that "peterborough pottery" generated 91 searches. Maybe "peterborough potter" would only generate two or three. Also, there were 110,000 searches for the phrase "pottery ceramic" and similar numbers for combinations of those two words. What does this all mean for my friend? (Or for you when you research your own terms?)

Clearly, she needs to have the word "pottery" on her website. And to make sure she captures the attention of local shoppers, she needs to repeat the phrase "Peterborough pottery" a few times. She should also pay attention to two-word combinations around "ceramics" and "pottery," as well.

What about "peterborough potter," though? Well, here's a suggestion. There could be anywhere from zero to nine people a month searching for the phrase "Peterborough potter." The fact that Google Maps found none means that my friend could easily own that phrase. How significant would that be? If someone is searching for a potter in Peterborough on Google Maps, and she is the only one to show up, it could mean two or three more sales a month. That could mean 24 to 36 more sales a year. I'd call that significant. And all she has to do to own that phrase is add a page to her website that talks about her as a potter and her potter experiences, and make sure she includes the term "potter" in her description on Google Places.

If she is smart, she will also add some references to "ceramics pottery" to both places, as well.

GOOGLE KEYWORD TOOL

Let's take a closer look at the Google Keyword Tool. You can easily find it if you go to Google and simply type "google keyword tool" into the search box. When you click on the link Keyword Tool – Google Adwords, it takes you to the sign-in page. If you look in the upper right-hand corner, you can see a button that says Sign In. If you have a Google Gmail account, go ahead and sign in. It only takes a few minutes to set up an account, and I recommend it, because it gives you some extended results with the keyword tool and you can avoid having to type in the "captcha" word each time. But if you don't want to create an account, no problem. You will still get up to 50 results for your searches.

For my example, I am going to do some searching around the term "toronto truck repair." To ensure my results are as local as possible, I am going to go to the highlighted Advanced Options and Filters line and click on Locations: United States x. That will activate the drop-down menu, and I can select Canada.

The reason I am using "toronto" is that with a larger city there will be more searches, and more variations of the main searches. Remember that Google doesn't show results for less than 10 searches? There are a lot of businesses where less than 10 searches could be significant. High-value purchases, like "truck repair" or "waterfront property" or "automobile" are examples of things you don't need to sell a whole lot of to have it affect your bottom line.

But repeat purchases, like "massage therapy" or "yard maintenance" or "hair salon" can have a high lifetime-customer value. A hair salon could add two customers a month, who stay with that salon for two years, and who spend $120 a year. That is a total sum of $5,760. If the salon used a website that costs three hundred bucks to put up and $120 a year to maintain, then they are getting a *one thousand percent* return on their marketing investment! This is a critical concepot and I explain it a little more fully in Appendix II. Please take the time to read this appendix because it could be worht thousands of dollars to you.

Let's go back to the keyword tool.

Here I've typed in "toronto truck repair." You can scroll down the list to see some of the results. About midway down this page, on the right side, you can see a little drop-down box. You can select how to rank the results of your search. In the example above, you can see that I have selected Global Monthly Searches. I want to know what are the most frequent keywords and keyword phrases used or associated with the concept "truck repair."

As you can see, "truck parts" is the most frequently used phrase. You can't see, but further down the page are the terms, "truck tire", "truck repair", "mobile repair service," and truck services," to name just a few.

Now, when someone goes looking for "truck tires," and you have made a point to include the phrase "repairs to truck tires" in the description of your business, Google is going to hook the two of you up. But if you haven't done the keyword research, it might not happen.

So, what can you do with keywords? If you have a website, you need to make sure you use your keywords in the text on the page. You should also use them in your domain name. If you can buy the domain "peterboroughtruckrepair.com" for your site, and the page title is Peterborough Truck Repair, and on that page you talk about "truck repair in Peterborough" and how customers can "get your truck repaired in Peterborough" and describe how you offer the "finest truck repair facility in Peterborugh," then Google will get the idea that when someone is searching for "peterborough truck repair" they should be shown your site high in the search engine rankings.

There are other factors that will affect your website search result placement, but these are among the most basic.

DIRECTORY LISTINGS

What happens if you don't have a website? Keyword research is still important. A lot of the results that Google shows to searchers are not websites. Google also shows directory listings.

When I do a search for "peterborough truck repair" on Google.ca, four of the top results are directories, iincluding Goldbook, Yellow Pages, and Super Pages.

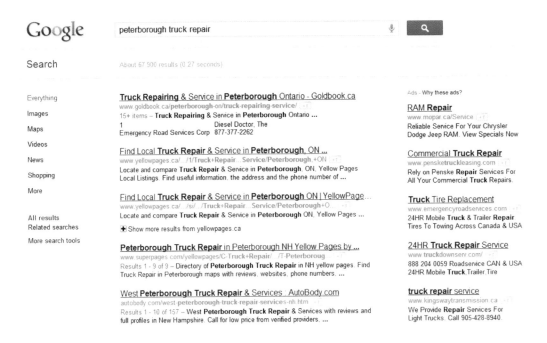

The directory listings that are shown will vary depending on the description of services that the owners have added. For instance, the results that come up after selecting yellowpages.ca are different if you include "truck tire," "truck repair," "mobile repair service," and truck services" in your business description than if you simply describe your business as "truck repair." Your business will tend to rank higher on the search engine results with more complete service options. That's probably better, if you are in the truck repair business.

The column of ads on the right-hand side of the page are from Google Adwords accounts. You need to have a good understanding of keyword results to use Adwords as well. I'm not going to get into that here, but I will say that those advertisers have instructed Google to have their ads shown when the phrase "peterborough truck repair" is searched for. They may also have instructed Google to only show the ads when someone within 30 miles of Peterborough uses that particular search. And they can limit the amount of money they spend each day on their advertising. As well, they only pay when someone actually clicks on their ads and goes through to their website. It is a very targetted form of advertising but a little advanced for general users.

There is another, and even more important, reason to do your keyword research. Google has given your business access to absolutely free Internet real estate. It is yours for the asking, and by doing things right, you can make a big impact on how many people find you when they go searching for your type of business or service in your area. In the next chapter we are going to talk about Google Places. It is critical that you read and absorb what is on the next few pages.

3 GOOGLE PLACES

Google has done something that is completely selfish on their part but great news for you. They have created a website for your business—for free. Or at least, if they haven't already created it, you can easily create one yourself, with Google's help. Take a look at the screen shot below:

Under the heading Places for roofers near Peterborough, ON, just above the start of the lettered placeholders, Google has listed seven items that it believes are legitimate roofers. I want you to notice something. Only one of those seven listings actually have their own websites, spelled out in light green text. All the rest say "maps.google.ca." These are the free websites Google has provided to try to give searchers the information they are looking for.

On another note, let's look at the so-called "organic" search results under the Google Places listings.

Peterborough Roofing Reviews - HomeStars **Peterborough**
30 Apr 2011 – Reviews of **Peterborough Roofing** companies. Homeowners share experiences on home contractors and retailers.
homestars.com/on/peterborough/roofing - Cached - Similar

Roofing Contractors in **Peterborough** Ontario - Goldbook.ca
Roofing Contractors in Peterborough Ontario - Goldbook.ca.
www.goldbook.ca/peterborough-on/roofing-contractors/ - Cached

Roofers, Roofing Installation **Peterborough** Ontario Canada
Roofers, Roofing Installation in Peterborough Ontario including **peterborough**, ontario, Roofers, Roofing Installation,, Harley Bower **Roofing**, Alf Curtis, ...
www.knowaboutnetwork.com/csb.php?cityid=2&cat=301 - Cached

Find Local **Roofers in Peterborough ON** | YellowPages.ca™
Locate and compare **Roofers** in Peterborough ON, Yellow Pages Local Listings. Find useful information, the address and the phone number of the local business ...
www.yellowpages.ca/search/si/1/**Roofers**/Peterborough+ON - Cached

Find BBB Accredited **Roofers** near **Peterborough, ON**
Find BBB Accredited **Roofers** near Peterborough, ON - your guide to trusted **Peterborough, ON Roofers**, recommended and BBB Accredited businesses.
www.bbb.org/ottawa/accredited-business.../roofing.../peterborough-on - Cached

Roofers in Peterborough - Local Peterborough Roofers
Fast responses and quality service can be expected from our reliable **Peterborough Roofers** when you visit localtraders.com.
www.localtraders.com/**roofers-in-peterborough**/ - United Kingdom - Cached - Similar

Peterborough Roofer | Roofing Contractor **Peterborough, ON**
Your Oshawa Roofer, Crowells **Roofing**, provides their **roofing** services in Peterborough, ON.
www.crowellsroofing.ca/on/Peterborough-roofer.html - Cached

Peterborough Roofing Company Ltd
Peterborough based **roofing** company offering its services to domestic and commercial clients.
www.peterboroughroofing.co.uk/ - Cached - Similar

Peterborough Roofing in Peterborough, ON - weblocal.ca
Peterborough Roofing at 1539 Chemong Rd, Peterborough, ON K9J 6X2.
www.weblocal.ca/peterborough-roofing-peterborough-on-1.html - Cached

Find Local **Roofing** Contractors in **Peterborough, ON** | Canpages ...
The best **Roofing** Contractors in **Peterborough** with reviews, maps, and contact information.
www.canpages.ca/.../peterborough/roofing.../3587-727400.html - Cached - Similar

Gooooooooogle ▶
1 2 3 4 5 6 7 8 9 10   Next

Organic search results are the unpaid search results that come up. Do you notice anything odd in the image? Only two of these results are actually roofers—and one of them is located in Peterborough in the United Kingdom!

All the rest are directory listings; yellowpages.ca, goldbook.ca, homestars.com, bbb.org, weblocal.ca, etc. are all directories. If you click on them, you have to then scroll down through their listings. Consumers often immediately back out of directory listings. They are looking for an individual roofer, not another list.

That means that on the first page of Google in a search for Peterborough Roofers (of which I found 21 listed as actually being in town), only eight show up. Seven of these results are in the Google Places listings. And five of those results have left their listings blank!

Now, does this seem like good marketing? Here's a no-cost way to be top of mind when someone goes looking for a roofer, and five out of seven businesses have done nothing. Don't you make the same mistake!

GET YOUR FREE LISTING

So, what do you need to do to claim your listing? It's easy. Go to Google.ca or Google.com. Type "google places" into the search box. Click on the first listing, or the one with the URL **www.google.ca/placesforbusiness** or **www.google.com/placesforbusiness.**

If you don't have a Google account, you will need to create one. This will take a few minutes, but is not a difficult process. Once you've completed it, you can sign up to claim your Places listing. The process is self-explanatory.

They will ask you to list your business phone and will populate your listing automatically with whatever information they find online. Here are a few important caveats. Before you create your listing, do a search for your business online using Google. You may already be listed in existing online trade directories, the online yellow pages, local chamber of commerce, etc. Google will be quite perturbed if you have conflicting information in different places—for instance, "123 Happy Lane" as opposed to "123 Happy Rd." Google sees discrepancies as an indication of a lack of legitimacy. Do yourself a favour, and correct and align any existing listings so they all show the same address, in the same format, with the same phone number, the same hours of operation, etc.

Frequently, owners of new businesses, particularly ones that started as part-time endeavours, will have different phone numbers in the various directories. I had one client who had three different numbers listed. He started out with his home number in a local business directory, then put down his cell number for the local Chamber of

Commerce listing, and then acquired a regular business phone when he located to a permanent storefront. So Google simply ignored his business for Google Maps.

Now, don't go rushing off to complete your listing just yet. When you do this, you'll want to do it right. Remember, you don't just want to claim your listing. Ideally you want to be in the number-one or number-two location. People tend to be a little lazy, and most folks will not bother going to page two of a Google search. Less than 10 percent of searchers make it to the second page. Sixty percent stop at the top three spots, so that's where you *really* want to be. How can you make that happen? Well, the answer is a little tricky.

I provided some Google Places listing advice to Sue, a friend who owns the "The Water Lily" in Hastings Ontario. Sue was careful with her descriptions and, even though she didn't completely fill in her Google Placers listing as completely as she might have, the results are very good.

The Water Lily comes up in top spots for searches in Hastings, but for searches in Campbellford, a larger town that is a fifteen minute drive away it also does very well, putting local Campbellford businesses to shame.

Sue's store ranks number two for "Coffee Shops near Campbellford", number two for "antiques near Campbellford", and number three for "clothing near Campbellford." She is beating out many larger retail outlets located right in Campbellford. Now imagine the possible impact of this on her business if vacationers renting cottages in the area are trying to decide what to do or where to go? Or if new residents located nearby are looking for services or retail outlets? Sue stands to gain from her efforts, while those whom she is beating out, or who have been pushed off the page by her listing are definitely going to lose.

GETTING TO THE TOP SPOT

Google is regularly changing the algorithms they use to do their online searches. Businesses are always looking for ways to land in the number-one spot, and every time someone comes up with a tricky way to do that, Google has to try to avoid the new trick. Google wants to reward the searchers by giving them relevant results. They definitely don't want to reward tricky marketers. In the past, the attitude of Google used to be, "If lots of other websites are pointing to a particular website, then the website they are pointing at must be pretty important." So webmasters and Internet marketers developed software that would pump out hundreds of websites in a few weeks. The websites they created were pretty dumb, but for a while they fooled

Google's search robots. Not anymore. Google does a pretty good job of figuring out what someone searching for "truck repair" is looking for. So what might that be?

Well, correct address is obvious. So is a telephone number, and a comprehensive description of services. Less obvious is a photograph of the outside of the shop. A photo makes it easier for the searcher to find, though, doesn't it? How about some photos of the inside of the shop, and maybe some before and after shots of body work? Google knows people like to watch videos these days, so if a business has a short one- or two-minute video explaining their services, Google gives them higher marks. In fact, Google allows you to upload up to ten photographs and four videos to your Google Places listing. Since almost no one does this, anyone who does is given more weight when Google presents the results of a search request.

So before you open your Google Places listing, put on your thinking cap, and get out your camera or have someone take the pictures for you. Ask yourself: If I were thinking about doing business here, what would I want to see?

I am sure you won't have any trouble taking 10 pictures that you don't mind sharing. The photos could be of work being done, work completed, facilities, products for sale in your store, or the end result of the work you do. A landscaper, renovator, or builder could highlight past projects. A real estate agent could show homes sold (with the sold sign). A baker could display products from the oven or decorated cakes. A restaurant could feature the menu or satisfied customers. Use a little imagination.

Think before you upload photo files called m102389.jpg. Keep your keyword search in mind when you name the individual files. Try file names like "Sold home in south Peterborough" or "decorated wedding cake" or "outdoor pond" or "renovated kitchen" or "selection of Pioneer chainsaws." I think you get the idea. Each time a keyword shows up in your Places listing, it helps Google decide which position your listing should occupy on the page. You don't want to just cram keywords in there, but labeling picture files in a way that describes content is justified.

Video is not much more complicated than that. If you have a digital camera, you have the ability to make a short one-minute video that will show clients your place of business, examples of your work, or simply you talking into the lens, explaining to them how you can help them get what they need and want.

A word of caution: Use a tripod or make sure the camera is resting on a solid surface while shooting the video. There's nothing wrong if it is obvious the video is amateur. It is the content that is important, after all. But there is no need to make the video look really *bad*.

To get your video into your Google Places listing, go to YouTube and sign up for an account. Browse to the location where your video file is stored—and upload. Once the file has been accepted, you will be given a unique URL identifying it. Copy that URL and paste it into the video url box in Google Places. That's it.

So let's go over everything again, in step-by-step form.

1. Do a search for your business online to see where you show up.
2. Check the accuracy of the information regarding address, phone, etc.
3. Copy the exact format down—for instance, if the existing info says "Street" then you don't want to say "St." in your Google Places listing. Don't list your cell phone if your main phone is already listed. You can always go back in a few weeks and add things, but let's not confuse Google in the beginning.
4. If you don't find any listings, create some. Add your business's info to existing local, regional, or national directories. That way, Google is assured you are a legitimate business when you ask for your listing. They will then give your listing more weight.
5. Do keyword research to determine how people are looking for your service/products.
6. Do take 10 pictures of various aspects of your business, customers, facilities, etc.
7. Rename the pictures using keywords as much as possible. At least use related terms.
8. Take a one-minute video. You can use Windows Movie Maker to create a video out of photographs.
9. Think about your description. Of course, incorporate the keywords, but also identify benefits for the customer.
10. Log in to Google Places and start filling in the information.
11. Upload the photographs. Think about the order you want them to appear in.
12. Upload the video
13. Submit.

Google will send you a postcard in about 1–2 weeks. It will have a PIN on it. For your Google Places listing to go live, you will need to log back in when you receive the postcard and enter the PIN. And that's it.

You can log in to your Google Places account and make a coupon available for people; you can let them know of upcoming specials or events, or you can go in and edit your information.

This is really only a few hours' work. It can have a significant impact on your business. Do you know what the lifetime value of one of your customers is? What would it mean to your business to get one extra customer a day, a week, or a month? It depends on what your average transaction is, of course, and how frequently your customers make additional purchases—but can you imagine what would happen if people were to go looking for your service and you were on the front page of Google instead of page two? What if you were in the first position instead of the fifth! It's up to you, of course, but a no-cost, three-hour expenditure of your time that will continue paying off for years sounds good to me.

GOOGLE PLACES ADVANCED

In a low-competition niche, the previous suggestions should get you to the top-seven listing for your selected keywords. But what happens if you're in hot competition with multiple other businesses? Things get a little more difficult and will require more effort on your part. But it still won't cost much money.

DIRECTORIES

I referred earlier to Google's propensity to provide searchers with relevant information. They want it to be relevant and correct. One way they do this is by validating any info they find. What is the content of the site? Are photographs and videos present? Do other websites refer to it? Is it listed in "authority sites?" What is an authority site? Well, the Better Business Bureau would be one. So would the local Chamber of Commerce. Google trusts that neither of these entities would allow scam artists to be listed in their respective sites or directories. Below is a list of respected business directories:

Yellow Pages	(http://www.yellowpages.ca)
Better Business Bureau	(http://www.bbb.org)
Canpages	(http://www.canpages.ca)
Thomson Local	(http:// w.thomsonlocal.com)
Connector Local	(http://www.connectorlocal.com)
Gold Book	(http://www.goldbook.ca)
411.ca	(http://www.411.ca)
Yelp	(http://www.yelp.com)
WorldWeb	(http://www.canada.worldweb.com)
CanadaOne	(http://www.canadaone.com)
Profile Canada	(http://www.profilecanada.com)
Scott's Directories	(http://www.scottsinfo.com)
FoundLocally	(http://www.foundlocally.com)
eSourceCanada	(http://www.esourcecanada.com)

CanLinks	(http://www.canlinks.net)
Canada Web Directory	(http://www.canadawebdir.com)
Shop In Canada	(http://www.shopincanada.com)
N49	(http://www.n49.ca)
AllPages	(http://www.on.allpages.com)

Suggestion: Open up Windows Notepad or WordPad. Type the info in there, and save that page to your desktop. Then, when the relatively tedious task of applying to all of the above directories is started, at least you can just cut and paste things like your business description, and you will consistently select the same categories.

Google will lend weight to appearances in these directories.

CITATIONS 1

Find your top competitors, or select any large city for a geo-search on Google Maps and type in your business or keyword phrase "in [large city name]." Take a look at the top listings, and copy down the company names. Now do a search in Google and see in which directories and other locations those company names come up. I'll show you what I mean.

The first listing is a paid advertisement. The next three are for the UK. But five of the next six listings are directories:

- homestars.com
- yellowpages.ca
- weblocal.ca
- thomsonlocal.com
- 192.com

The top result for the Google Maps search for "roofing near peterborough ON" was Peterborough Roofing. A search for "Peterborough Roofing" turned up their listings in these five directories. If you were a Peterborough roofer, you would want to make sure you were listed in at least these directories as well.

CITATIONS 2

There's another way to get citations for your business—video sharing sites. When you upload a video to YouTube, make sure you fill out the description, starting with your vital business information. This is crawlable by the search engine spiders. It will be more proof of the legitimacy of your business.

Other video listing sites are Vimeo and Daily Motion. They all make room for you to include a short description, and that description needs to contain your business name, address and phone number, plus website if you have one.

Making a video isn't hard. You can use Microsoft Movie Maker, which probably came

loaded on your computer.

See Appendix 1 for the straightforward instructions.

Another alternative is to simply create a slide presentation in PowerPoint from Microsoft Office 2010 and export it as an MP4 file. You can easily add audio to provide narration, or just stick with text.

CITATIONS 3

Remember those 10 photographs you took? Well, a good strategy to follow is to have them uploaded to a free photo-sharing site. Two of the best are Flickr and Photobucket. Make sure to set your access to "public" and add tags to your photo—both subject matter (think keyword) and geo-identifier. So a kitchen renovation in Campbellford might be tagged "Campbellford granite countertop" or "Campbellford kitchen renovation." When you are filling out your Google Places listing, instead of uploading them directly, you list their urls, and your Google Places listing will still show them.

REVIEWS

Reviews are extremely important for good placement on Google Maps listings, but more to the point is something you can see on the screen shot below.

The two listings above with more than five reviews jump out at you. Google rewards businesses having five or more reviews with the multiple-star designations. Something else you should know: Google puts more weight behind reviews from third-party locations than from its own listing service. Google actively crawls and notes reviews on:

- ca.local.yahoo.com
- yelp.ca
- restaurantica.com
- Service Magic
- …and others.

You will see these reviews when you click on a business's Places listing. Below are examples of reviews for a Peterborough restaurant called Night Kitchen.

Reviews from around the web

restaurantica.com - 16 reviews ★★★★☆

"The best place to get pizza in peterborough. Delicious **pizza** thats still healthy in lots of interesting choices vegan and vegetarian friendly. Great laidback atmosphere on a great street. The staff have always been friendly and helpful and its very reasonably priced." - Aug 15, 2009

> **"Ya gotta love their pizza.** I have a friend who is lactose intolerant, and she loves the fact that they always have vegan **pizza** options. Great for lunch, and goes down really well after the bar. I love that it's pleasing to look at, tastes wonderful and is not ..." - Sep 12, 2008
> www.restaurantica.com/on/peterborough/the.../23004496/

yelp.ca ★★★★★

"We love the Night Kitchen pizzas!! ! They are thin crust the way we like them and the combinations and toppings are inventive! It's a tiny place with a handful of stools alone the window so a slice or take-out is your best bet. Funky and fun, just like a **pizza** joint should be!" - Aug 22, 2010
www.yelp.ca/biz/night-kitchen-the-speclty-pizza-peterborough

happycow.net ★★★★☆

"Night Kitchen is amazing! They have so many veg options, including vegan options. My whole family (I'm the only vegan, the rest are omni) loves to get their **pizza**. My favorite has tomato sauce, sweet potato, eggplant, and caramelized onions. They only serve thin ..." - Jul 11, 2010
www.happycow.net/reviews.php?id=6313

Reviews by Google users

Been here? Rate and review

jaff - Feb 4, 2011
★★★★★ **AMAZING pizza!** Best anywhere! I love this place, I HIGHLY recommend it! Awesome food, great atmosphere, perfectly priced and friendly cashiers!! I RATE THIS ABOVE FIVE STARS!!!!
Liked: Food, Service, Atmosphere, Value
Was this review helpful? Yes - No - Flag as inappropriate

hedgren - Nov 22, 2010
★★★★☆
Flag as inappropriate

Do not—I repeat, DO NOT—sit at your computer and put in multiple reviews for your own business, or have your friends create different log-in identities and put in multiple reviews. Do not have two people put in reviews from the same computer. Google can identify which IP address a review came in from. Google will suspend your account if it believes you have been trying to trick it.

Having said that, encourage customers, friends, or anyone you can think of to put in honest reviews, from different review sites, on different occasions. Google will pick up on it if there are a flood of reviews one week and nothing the next two. So play by the rules.

Here's another thought. If you have a pile of phony positive reviews up on your Google Places listing, and someone reads them and then is really disappointed, that person may very well strike out at the business by putting a particularly nasty review up there. You can't stop him or her. You really don't want to encourage that kind of reaction.

Something else to consider. If you have a bunch of friends put up single reviews for your business, and those same friends haven't been putting up reviews on other businesses, they will be given less weight. A consumer who has been leaving reviews for local businesses for some time, and has 20 other reviews out there will count much more heavily, for obvious reasons.

Once you do have reviews up on the web at yelp.ca or Yahoo, you can use the More Details section at the bottom of the Google Listing page.

| See our Reviews on restaurantica.com | : | http://www.restaurantica.com/on/peterborough |
| See our Reviews on yelp.ca | : | http://www.yelp.ca/biz |

COUPONS

Google likes to see coupons being used, or rather; I should say they interpret the presence of coupons as of interest to potential customers, so they lend some importance to their presence. The coupon can be for whatever you want—extended guarantee, free consultation, 5 percent off, whatever. They do need to be renewed periodically.

SUMMARY

Google Places provides a free and effective way to get your business information out there for your customers and prospects. It allows you to own a piece of Internet real estate without spending any money at all. Of course, there are services that will list your businesses on Google for you and take the necessary steps to optimize your Places listing for maximum effect, saving you the time and extending your reach by working to get you a higher-ranked listing. No service can guarantee you a long-term number-one ranking in Google, because Google changes its algorithms all the time. But a service like mine will, at the very least, make sure it is done correctly according to the latest industry insider information, and it will save you a significant amount of time, simply because of experience.

Your Places listing doesn't have to be where you stop, however. Many businesses already have websites, and it doesn't have to be difficult or expensive to acquire one. In the next section of this guide I will go over how you can use your website in concert with your Google Places listing to more effectively market your business and maintain that all-important relationship with your customer.

4 EMAIL MARKETING

I was going to leave this item till later, but it is so important that I want to talk about it now. Email marketing is the easiest, cheapest way to increase your revenue that has ever been created. Industry experts claim an average return on investment of 50 to 1. There are very few things you can do that even come close to this.

People buy what you have to sell because you are offering them something that meets a need or a want at the time they decide to move on it. They have decided on you as the supplier either because of proximity, convenience or because they have a higher level of trust and respect in you as a potential supplier of their need.

You can run ads every week in the newspaper, but for the vast majority of the time, those ads are wasted because people seeing them don't want what you are selling right then. People have also learned how to ignore ads in most media, the best example being the folks that fast forward through their video recordings of TV shows when the commercials show up, using their PVR's or VHS machine (yes, people still record TV shows on VHS tapes).

What could be better for your business than to have a private list of customers that want to hear what you have to say on a weekly basis? They want to hear about new products, how to best use the products they have bought from you, and they want to hear about opportunities to buy from you again. That is the power of email marketing and the two best things about it are that it is almost free, and you can automate the process so it works for you on a regular basis with almost no input.

You can send people to a web page, have them fill out a short form and then they can receive a series of emails for the next year that you have written ahead of time. Every time a new customer signs up, they receive the same sequence of emails, even years into the future, but you only had to write them once (or have someone write them for you).

Getting people to give you their email requires you to give them something in exchange, but that doesn't have to be difficult. If they know that they will be receiving advance notice of specials or discounts, that might be enough to get them to sign up. If you had a special report or audio or video, showing them how to do something, get more value from products you sell, or use them in special ways, that might be enough.

For example, if you sold gas powered equipment, like lawn mowers, trimmers, generators, etc. you could produce a 6-10 page report on the best way to maintain that equipment. You could offer it for free if they subscribe to your email list. They could go to a simple web page to download it and then they would automatically start receiving emails from the autoresponder that you have setup.

There are places you can go where reports and documents are available for free. How about one like this, on yard maintenance: "Ecological Landscaping Tools for Homeowners," a fifty page report I found with just a few minutes searching online.

Aweber is one service that will allow you to manage an email list this way. There is a monthly fee, but it has free training, resources, suggestions on email marketing and is a trusted service that will help prevent spam filters from stopping your emails.

Maintaining an email list doesn't have to be a large burden. In fact shorter messages are better. Keeping customers informed of what is going on with your business doesn't take a great effort. Informing them of the highlights in your weekly newspaper flyer will help prevent it from getting thrown away without a glance.

You can pass on the location of an extremely useful website or inform them of a local event that you know about and that relates to your shared interest. If you were a grocery store owner and you knew of a cooking class that was coming up, it would make sense for you to mention it, maybe along with the fact that you stock supplies for that particular cuisine in aisle six of your store. You can reference events involving sports or other organizations that you sponsor, casually reminding customers of your involvement in community events.

The beauty of Aweber, or other autoresponder services, is that you can program them to send out a specific sequence of emails that are prewritten, and also send out fresh timely information. Everyone that signs up with you gets emails number one through ten in sequence.

Let's say you are that grocery store owner. Someone has signed up and they get the following emails in sequence. Email number one welcomes them to your list, lets them know how frequently to expect emails from you and gives them some information on what to expect in the coming months. Email number two tells them about a great website that offers information on something they can use. In between emails number two and three, you send out a special email telling all your customers that some product rep is going to be in the store offering samples of their wares and people should be there on Saturday morning if they are interested.

Back in sequence now, email number three lets them know that some product they have in their home can be used in this new and unique way. Email number four lets them know that not only do you sell food but you will put together party trays and you do some simple catering. Email number five lists the best and cheapest time to buy seasonal products, suggesting that they might want to consider this in planning their menus or shopping. You send out another blast to all customers about a special bulk order you have made that will allow you to offer some product at a reduced price.

What is really happening now is that people are looking forward to your messages. You are offering valuable information that they want and can use. Every once in a while you are slipping in something that is a straight marketing shot. But they are generally happy to get it because they might need it and they appreciate knowing in advance. Because of the weighting of value to marketing, they are okay with the marketing. The same thing happens in a newspaper doesn't it? People put up with the advertising because that's the price of getting the news. And every once in a while the advertising is exactly what they want. But they have to put up with a lot of advertising they don't want.

The retiree doesn't care about kid friendly yards in a new housing development. The townie doesn't care about farm equipment. The avid bird watcher isn't concerned about performance equipment for their street rod (usually) and the economy car owner isn't paying a lot of attention to advertisements for heavy duty suspensions for people that want to tow their vacation homes around the country.

When people sign up for your email list, you are in the lucky position of preaching to the converted. They are already on your side and they want to hear your message.

How Do You Get Sign-ups?

There are lots of zero and low cost ways to get people to sign up to your list. You can have a message on your sales slip directing them to a web subscription form. Services like Aweber make this straightforward and show you how to do it. All of your advertising graphics and messages should invite people to that web location to sign up. You could offer something to get their email address. A report or eBook, as I suggest above. You could have a video or audio recording that they can download after signing up. You could have a book printed up and let people know that the book is available for pick up at your business once they have joined you list. You could have a special deal for list members only that allows them to gain store credit when they make a purchase. Something similar to the "fee coffee" cards some coffee shops use. Ten cups of coffee bought earns you a free one.

An excellent way to get subscribers to your list is to get in touch with others who already have a list and are in a related field of area of interest. You can then let people on his or her list know of your free book, frequent buyers bonuses, special exclusive membership list, one time 50% discount on a particular item or whatever. You could gain automatic exposure to hundreds of potential new subscribers if you have something of value to offer that other list owners' members. And that list owner gets an opportunity to send an email out to his or her subscribers that offers real value.

If you don't know any businesses that already have a list, maybe you should get in touch with some local business owners and figure this process out and get started building your respective lists.

It can take multiple contacts between you and a prospect before they commit to the point of making a purchase. Once a purchase is made, however, the likelihood of them purchasing again goes way up. With an email list, you have multiple opportunities to impress them with your honesty, credibility, expertise, and simple customer caring attitude. Moving them from there to an actual purchase becomes almost straightforward.

In Appendix 2 I talk about the lifetime value of a customer. You need to think about this when you decide if managing an email list is worth your time and effort. Remember, you are not committing fifteen minutes a week to each of you customers. You are committing fifteen minutes a week to all of them at once, making them more loyal, more responsive and perhaps convincing them to buy more frequently.

Outside of getting your Google Places listing up and working effectively for you, email marketing is the most effective thing you can do to boost the number and responsiveness of your customers. If you are not using email to market effectively, you are leaving money on the table, a lot of money. Remember, you are already stuck with your existing costs for overhead, staff, and ongoing marketing. If you put in eight hours setting up your email autoresponder, and then invested an additional fifteen minutes a week, or twelve hours a year and it gave you a 5% increase in revenue, would it be worth it?

5 WEBSITES AND WHAT THEY NEED

This is a huge topic, and you can go out and buy four-hundred-page books that discuss websites. Have you noticed that many websites are in a terrible state? There are numerous simple things you can do (or arrange to have done) to make yours better. You need to first determine what the purpose is of your website. Is it a replacement for a brochure—that is, a picture of the outside and maybe the inside of your business? A few shots of products? Store hours and an address and telephone number?

That's okay, and it will be of some use to people. But it could be so much more.

One of the best uses of a website is to generate leads. To do that, you need to capture email addresses or telephone numbers (email addresses are far easier to capture). Encouraging people to accept a free white paper or short report explaining some issue they should be aware of helps position you as a local expert—and an obvious choice if they need assistance in that area.

A website is also a great place for photo galleries if you have an extensive product line.

A testimonials page, where potential buyers can see real, live people (endorsements from Judy M. in Stirling won't cut it). Even better, video endorsements from your customers have greater impact.

Staying on the video theme, demonstrations of how to use products you sell, or informational videos about your products or services, will explain why they are desirable.

So, what is it you want to do?

GETTING FOUND

How do you make sure you show up on the Internet? Too many websites are like the billboard in the illustration below; they are in a place with no traffic. One of the best sources of traffic is that which flows to your site naturally when you show up in Google's search results. So how can you get that? Keep reading!

KEYWORDS

Ideally, your website (or Google Places page) will come up when someone does a search on some specific keywords. That is far more likely to happen if you have made sure that the keywords are on your page. A haphazard arrangement will not do. It could get you penalized by Google. Ideally your keyword appears in your domain name. It's even better if your domain name includes a geo-identifier. All things being equal, WarkworthDentist.com will work better for a Warkworth dentist then BobSmith.com.

You want the title of your page to have the keywords in it as well—and the first few words of the first sentence. Google's search engines then see a certain alignment of information. Sticking with the dentistry theme, the page title you are trying to optimize could be "Your Warkworth Dentist." Your first sentence could be: "Warkworth dentist? You don't have to look far. Bob Smith has been practising dentistry in Warkworth for 20 years."

Any page should have a main keyword or keyword phrase and one or two secondary phrases. These should appear early, in the first sentence or two, as in the example above, and then they should be repeated a few times on the page. A too-frequent occurrence will be seen by Google as an attempt to trick the search engines, and the page will be rejected. A keyword density of around 3 percent will be safe and effective.

TAGS

Your website developer has probably taken care of the title tags and Meta tags on your site. I won't get into a technical discussion here that is too complicated for the length of this guide, but I will mention something that is often missed. If you go to a website (I did a quick search for Rice Lake Cottages and came up with a rental cottage site) you might find a picture like the one below.

The url for this image is
http://www.alpineresort.ca/images/2008/IMG_3920.jpg

It does have an alt tag, which is "Kevin's bass."

You could see this information if you put your mouse cursor on the picture and right clicked, then selected "copy image url" and pasted it into notepad.

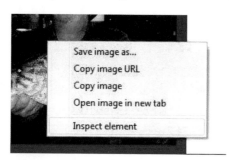

Likewise, if you right clicked and selected Inspect Element, you would get a bunch of HTML code, with the picture element highlighted, as below.

```
▼<td>
    <img src="images/2008/IMG_3920.jpg" alt="Kevin's bass" width="250" height="250">
  </td>
```

There you see the URL and also the alt text. So here is the point of all this discussion of tags and urls. Google does not penalize you for the appearance of your keywords as part of your image descriptions. Instead of having that image labeled with the name given it by the camera, "IMG 3920.jpg," you could rename it "Kevins Rice Lake Bass.jpg." The alt text could be the same: "Kevins Rice Lake Bass." That is grist for the search engine mill. You could also call the image "[name of resort rental cottages] bass.jpg." Both of those alternative names would help attract attention whenever someone is searching for Rice Lake bass—or the name of the resort—or rental cottages on Rice Lake!

CONTENT

Google wants to make the searcher's experience a fruitful and pleasant one, so they want to deliver material they believe will meet the searcher's needs. If someone is looking for "how to grow nut trees" and your Ontario Hybrid Nut Tree site has pages of information, links to other sites about nut trees, photographs, downloadable documents, and videos showing planting and grafting procedures, your site is going to appear.

Content can appear to be an insurmountable task to anyone who is not used to writing. But it doesn't have to be. Content that people will link to is the best kind, and one of the easiest ways to achieve both content creation and linking is to generate lists. People love linking to resources, and blog writers on other sites regularly post website addresses for their readers to look at and use. So think about lists you could create. These could be lists of other websites that provide information, or lists of places that can supply needs your own establishment can't fill, or lists of how to do something step by step. They could be resource or materials lists for projects. All are fair game and not difficult to put together.

There are also many places on the Internet where you can get public-domain information free. Everything from plans for chicken coops to films is available in the public domain and is free to use as content on your website.

We have discussed many of the actions you can take to improve the likelihood of your website getting found in the section on Google Places. In fact, most of the items discussed in this guide allow for you to mention your website. Videos, documents, articles, Facebook pages, signature files in forum and blog posts and comments—any and all of these will drive traffic back to your website and also create links that raise its profile.

Unfortunately, the most recent change in Google's system of ranking has given websites much more clout than previously. Google has decided that a business without a website isn't as serious as a business that has one. Their reasoning is that a website can provide much more information to the consumer (searcher) and is more likely to satisfy that person's needs.

A website doesn't have to be complicated. Even a one-page brochure site or Facebook Fan Page will help here. As long as it duplicates the business information and has the primary keywords included, it will raise the status of your Google listing. Of course, all things being equal, the more relevant content on the site, the more relevant the site is, as far as Google is concerned—but the quality of the site is only one factor that Google considers. So don't let that stop you.

This will work well in concert with the strategy of making sure your business has citations in the appropriate directories, etc. All of those other locations have places to include a website address. So your citations can serve a dual purpose. They have the business address, validating you for Google, and they provide backlinks to your website, raising your website's importance in Google's eyes. And the more important your website, the more highly ranked your Google Places listing will be when it comes up as a search result.

Further to your website's backlinks, make sure that if you do have one or get one, it is linked to and from other websites in your area. Examples of places to get desirable links would be the local Chamber of Commerce, local Business Associations, any city or county portals or directory sites, regional commercial associations, and local newspaper or news websites.

BACKLINKS

I've mentioned several times in this report how important backlinks can be. In past simpler times (10 years ago) Google paid most of their attention to backlinks. The premise was that if a lot of websites were linking to a particular website, then that website must be pretty important or at least have lots of great information or services available on it. What happened over the years is that people looking to make fast money automated the website-creation process and found ways to create dozens of websites a day. In a few weeks it was possible to create hundreds of websites, full of nonsense or barely readable text all pointing to the website you wanted to promote. People searching the Internet for information were coming up with garbage results.

Of course, this immediately threatened Google's business model, and they took steps to penalize these "spam" websites. Now it is very hard to sneak this kind of phony website past the Google search engine algorithms. Google's focus now is even more rigorously on content. But that is okay. No one is going to argue with the value of the content on legitimate websites. So, if you can get valid links from real sites, it will continue to help Google recognize the validity of your site.

The point here is: The more places that link to your website—if they are related!—the better. There is no point in getting your brother's highly ranked dog-training website to link to your flower shop. In fact, it could hurt.

There are various completely legitimate things you can do to benefit your website's ranking with backlinks. I'm going to go down a list and explain them to you one at a time.

COMMENTS

Pretty much every community and interest group in existence now has a blog, forum, or community portal, where they can discuss issues and topics of common interest. Many of these blogs and forums allow readers to make comments. Whether it's the Arts Northumberland or Northumberland Views site, if you have something useful to add, or suggestions or questions about the posts of articles you have read in them, there may be an opportunity for you to get a backlink. Of course, one way is to simply mention that people can find more information about a topic being discussed by referring them to an appropriate page on your website. But even if you don't do that, it is quite common for a person to write his or her name at the bottom of a post and put a website address directly below. That website address can become a link back to your website. It also adds credibility to your comment, because you are not simply someone expressing an opinion but a businessperson, with a vested interest in maintaining a reputation for honesty and service. Unsaid in this is that your comment must actually have some value and not simply be an excuse to get your website's name out there. Posting a message that says "Good point. Joe Shirley Businessperson, MyWebsite.com" will pretty soon be seen as nothing more than "comment spam" and will likely be removed or even have you blocked from commenting.

You can use Google to help you find places to comment. Go to the Google home page. In the upper left corner you can see the list of specific searches: Web, Images, Video, etc. Click on More and select Blogs from the drop-down menu. Add your topic area and location modifier for a possible list of appropriate blogs.

You can also try searching for your chosen topic followed by the word "forum." Just remember to read the rules, and don't make a three-word comment followed by your backlink. Add something of value, or post an opinion or some advice. In fact, you are better off simply picking a few places that look good and then making a habit of reading the posts to get a feel for what they have to offer.

This is a process, not a one-shot. If you read the new posts on five or six different forums or blogs, it won't take more than a half an hour of your time a week. And when you make comments, you are adding backlinks and building your own reputation and that of your business. After a few months of this, you will have added significantly to your site's standing in Google's eyes, and a move from page two of the search results to page one could have a huge impact in your business. It's time well spent— not to mention that you will be getting a real look at your local customers' concerns.

ARTICLES

If you have knowledge in a particular field related to your business (and I assume you do have or you wouldn't be in business), then you can automatically get links back to your site. If you have writing ability, then you can submit even a short article, 350–500 words long, to one or more of the numerous article sites online. Typically you need to register for these sites, and when you do you create a little information box that is attached to each of your articles. In that information box is a clickable link to your website.

Article-Listing Directories:

ezinarticles.com

squidoo.com

hubpages.com

technorati.com

buzzle.com

suite101.com

brighthub.com

goarticles.com

isnare.com

gather.com

Article-sharing sites recently took a hit in importance because, as you would expect as soon as Search Engine Optimization (SEO) gurus realized how much attention Google was paying to them, they started cranking out articles. They used outsourced writers from India and Asia who would write articles for a few bucks each. They even developed software that would "spin" written articles by substituting synonyms for many of the words in the articles to automatically create new versions. In this way, they could pay for one article and then create a dozen more out of it, all of which were automatically submitted to hundreds of article-sharing sites. Of course, in a very short time Google was bringing up search results that had great page rankings, because of backlinks, but the value of the search results weren't based on anything of real value.

This doesn't mean that articles are now worthless. Well-written articles will attract real attention from human eyeballs, so your site will get traffic as a result. And the same articles can be sent to owners of niche blogs as a way of introducing your knowledge and writing skill. Your article could lead to an invitation to write a guest blog post.

Another category of sharing sites are those featuring documents. The submissions at these sites are typically longer and more scholarly, but don't let that scare you off. The key is useable information. As long as your writing is readable, it will get read. People are looking for information, not Shakespeare.

DOCUMENT SHARING

1. **http://www.scribd.com/**
2. **http://www.docstoc.com/**
3. **http://www.4shared.com/**
4. **http://www.docshare.com/**
5. **http://www.wepapers.com/**

You might be saying to yourself, "I can't write," and maybe it's true—but there are numerous ways to get an article done. You could come up with a list of questions about your business or the area your business operates in. Then just answer the questions. Lists are also great. "What five things can I do to help prevent water from leaking into my basement?" You could ask your spouse or a friend to interview you about your business or business area and then take notes about the answers. The notes become an outline for your article(s). You could do some research on the Internet (or have one of your school-age children do it) and use the information you find as an outline of what to say.

Don't think of this kind of strategy as an all-or-nothing effort. Think of it more as a work in progress. If you aimed for a 350-word article every two weeks, in a year you would have more than 25 article or document links pointing back to your site. These articles and documents frequently get picked up and posted at other locations around the web. Those 25 articles could turn into 30, 40, or 50 backlinks if webmasters like your writing and feature the articles on their own blogs.

6 SOCIAL MEDIA

Social media are a whole story on their own, and I will talk about what you can do with them in a little bit. But I just want to remind you that Facebook, Twitter, etc., are all great places to place links to your website, and it happens completely naturally when you are engaged with your customers or clients on any of the social media sites.

Social media has been around long enough now that it can hardly be called new, but it definitely is new for many small businesses. Social media can seem confusing and amorphous, hard to get hold of. Aren't social media sites just places for people to share photographs, put up inane posts about what thoughts just flitted through their heads or share links to different YouTube videos they "liked"?

Not exactly. At their best, they allow people to create a community. It's not the same as the neighbourhood you grew up in, but it approaches the feeling of a circle of friends. And for a business, it doesn't really get much better than that.

The poster child of social media today is Facebook. Facebook is a social-networking site that was launched in February 2004. By January 2011 it had garnered over six-hundred-million users. It is now considered the third-largest web-based company in the United States—after Google and Amazon—and usually has more visitors every day than Google.

Imagine that someone has a great experience at your place of business. Then the next day over coffee, they tell two of their friends at work. You would like that. Better yet, imagine that they said, "I absolutely put my stamp of approval on that business." You would *really* like that. Now imagine they told 236 of their closest friends that that was how they felt about your business. Well, that's what social media like Facebook and Twitter can be. People are regularly sharing their "likes" with their entire roster of friends.

Facebook is definitely not just for kids anymore. The registration statistics show this. The number of new members between the ages of 35 and 55 has grown at an astounding 277 percent in the last year, while the 55+ age group has shown a remarkable 195 percent increase in new registrations. This is definite proof that the "young" sheen has worn out of Facebook.

SOCIAL MEDIA BENEFITS

The benefits of social media are many, and they can translate directly to the bottom line. Let's list some:

They help you stand out from your competitors—particularly if your competitors are *not* using social media. It is a noisy online world out there. Competition from national brands and large corporations is intense. More and more it encroaches on the domain of small business, with increased customization and delivery speed, and low price. When you take your small business online into the social-media maelstrom, it is easier for your customers to take you along for the ride.

An increase in search engine rankings is virtually automatic. As your Facebook Fan Page accumulates "likes," and your fans link back to your comments and posts, your rising fan page will lift your webpage with it.

Brand familiarity is easier to achieve if you are part of the Facebook community and you are engaging people. Compare your situation to your competitor who is not on Facebook. You are making posts that are picked up by people's news feeds. They are "liking" your page or your comments. Their friends are seeing their likes and responses to your comments. And your competitor is never mentioned.

Increased traffic is almost automatic, as well. At least some of the people who see their friends "liking" you will click through to your fan page and/or your website. Once they are there, you can offer them reasons to subscribe to your email list by offering access to discounts or bonuses. Once they are on your email list, communication becomes easier.

Increased traffic to your website and more subscribers to your email list of prospects and customers mean that your marketing reach is greater. People feel closer to other people who are engaged in their community. Social media helps businesses approach this kind of engagement. New posts on your fan page or new tweets don't seem like spam, as long as you aren't obviously selling something. Social media is mostly about sharing and giving, so you can't expect direct sales from your posts. However, posts or tweets that send people to your website for a look have a higher chance of leading to a direct sales piece.

Market research is easier on Facebook, because people there are already used to responding to comments—and responding is unbelievably easy. It's almost like asking questions at a party, as opposed to conducting a telephone survey.

New business partnerships can result from social media exposure. Same-market, non-competitive businesses can find each other and partner as a result of social media.

Another benefit is more trust. Because of the higher level of engagement and the increased social proof that occurs every time someone "likes" your fan page, the trust factor is higher. Think about it. A potential customer lands on your fan page and sees that 237 other people "like" your page. That is social proof—a pile of mini-testimonials if you like (see image below).

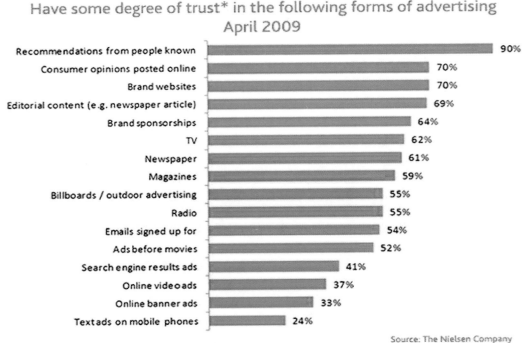

Have some degree of trust* in the following forms of advertising
April 2009

Form of advertising	Percentage
Recommendations from people known	90%
Consumer opinions posted online	70%
Brand websites	70%
Editorial content (e.g. newspaper article)	69%
Brand sponsorships	64%
TV	62%
Newspaper	61%
Magazines	59%
Billboards / outdoor advertising	55%
Radio	55%
Emails signed up for	54%
Ads before movies	52%
Search engine results ads	41%
Online video ads	37%
Online banner ads	33%
Text ads on mobile phones	24%

Source: The Nielsen Company
*E.g. 90 percent of respondents trusted "completely" or "somewhat" recommendations from people they know

As you look at the chart, one thing jumps out. Recommendations from friends carry almost 30 percent more weight than newspaper editorial content. Even anonymous consumer opinions posted online carry more weight than newspaper editorials. Think about that! How much do you love getting free publicity from a friendly newspaper article about your business? And that happens how often? And then it is relegated to the litter box. A "like" is there for all time. You need to be getting some of that.

1. An additional point of contact that allows connections. Simply because of the nature of social media it will be almost impossible to stop some personality leaking through to your interaction with the people who make up your market. Indeed, it is highly desirable. People can't connect with a business or a website. They can connect with an individual. How often are

you likely to see someone at your place of business? Compare that to how often they will see your posts online if they become one of your fan pages friends. (Every time you post they will see it.)

2. There are elements of this in the above, but it is worthy of a separate mention: Facebook and other media provide you with free promotion. It involves time, either yours or someone else's, but that is controllable by you. A few sessions a week, taking 10–15 minutes of your time each session, can elicit all of the benefits mentioned above.

HOW DO YOU USE SOCIAL MEDIA?

Here's a short summary of how something spreads across the net through social media.

You create a fan page or business page. You let people in your email contacts know about it and invite them to check it out.

You post a useful bit of information in your field of expertise that can help someone save money, make money, prevent a mistake, or help them have more fun. It could be a couple of paragraphs or even just a link to a page on your blog or website. The key thing here is it must be useful. This does not mean a lead to a sale of some item you will make money from.

Your Facebook page has 10 people who are following it. Three of these people go to your page because they saw a little clip of the post. Two of them actually use the info and either save money, make money, prevent an accident, or have crazy fun. They both immediately send a blast out to all their friends—let's say a total of 150 people. A total of 26 of these people are intrigued enough to visit your page, and a higher percentage of them follow the advice (because their friends have already tried and been successful at using it), so 12 of them try your suggestion. Positive results follow for 10 of them, and they immediately send blasts out to their friends. Now one thousand people receive the info … and so on … and so on. In a short time, really useful, lucrative, or funny clips or posts can make the rounds to thousands and thousands of people.

Now, in most cases, this will be geographically limited, in terms of benefit to you. Someone from New Zealand might receive the post but will likely never buy anything from you. But this doesn't matter too much. You can still personally benefit from having that person like you, because your "like" count just went up, and every "like" is social proof of the usefulness and trust factor associated with your page and you.

Facebook makes it easy for people to share, and that makes it different from a website.

Suddenly, instead of a static webpage, which isn't much different from a brochure that friends can pass around, people are engaged in a conversation. They can see each other's reaction to this new web location. They get notifications about their (and your) activities on that location and are now active instead of just passive observers.

GETTING STARTED

Use your Internet browser to log on to the Internet, and go up to the browser's location bar and type in "facebook.com/pages." In the upper right-hand section of the page you will see a box with the text "Create Page" in it.

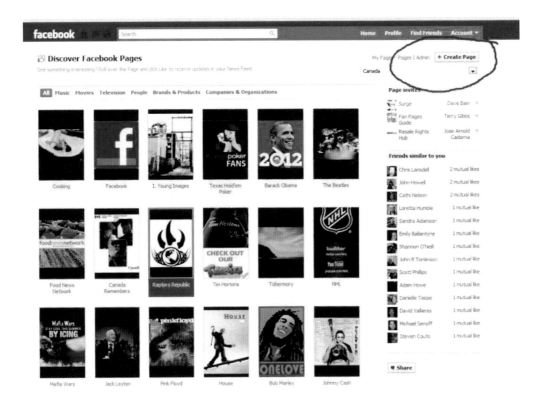

Go ahead and click on "Create Page." You'll next be taken to a page where you can select the type of Facebook page you wish to create

Connect with your fans on Facebook.

Local Business or Place

. There are several different options, which have different implications, but there is no need to get fancy. Just select Local Business or Place.

Then you can begin to input some simple information. Once you are done, you have to agree to Facebook's Pages Terms. Click on Get Started.

You are now looking at your basic page layout. It is a little short on info, but that is what you can now correct. In the upper right-hand corner is an Edit Page button. Select this and you will be given an opportunity to expand your description by including store hours and specifying what you do and what you provide.

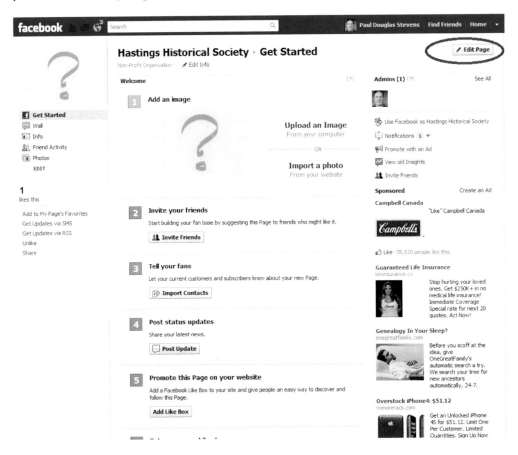

Fill out the blank spaces, and pay attention to your description. Remember the keyword research you did? Your description needs to include those keywords. The terms that people use when searching are what will resonate with them.

There is space here for your email address and also for your website. Be sure to include them.

You are just about done. Only a few more details to take care of. We've talked about the social nature of Facebook and other social media. Think of them as an ongoing conversation, just as you have with your friends. When you are apart from friends, you don't have to start all over again when you meet again. You just pick up where you left off. Aim for that same level of relaxation, but recognize that you are a professional, representing your business. So relaxed is okay, but completely informal is not.

Upload a photo that can be used to represent your business. Your logo is perfect. If you have a website, you can probably grab an image from it. Otherwise, a photo of the storefront or your sign could work.

Time to put in your first status update. Nothing fancy required—it is just important to get a few posts up before you invite any friends to like your page. An announcement of an upcoming special, sale, appearance, or the introduction of a new staff member or a new product line would all be fine. Alternatively, a short hello from you and an invitation for people to come back to see news and upcoming events at your store would work.

Notice the little icons right under your page name: Status, Photo, Link, Video, and Question? They provide easy-to-use ways to add content to your page. The way that you use them will determine how successful your page will be. Remember, your main focus on this page is your customers, not your store. How can you add value in your relationship to them? How can you help them? What might they want to see?

Again, there's no need to be crazy and put yourself through some kind of exhausting third degree every time you add content. There is nothing wrong with having some fun. Some shots of the company barbeque are okay. It will help your business staff seem more like an organization of real people instead of a faceless commercial enterprise. But remember to think in terms of your customers, and you won't go far wrong.

7 CONCLUSION

I hope this guide has demystified the whole process of using the Internet. The web has put tremendous power in the hands of any small business or individual who chooses to make use of it. It seems complicated at first, but when you take it one step at a time and keep focused on each task until it is done and you can move on to the next, it becomes far less intimidating.

There are numerous resources online to help you go beyond the surface treatment I have provided in this short book. Of course, there are also many service people you can hire to do the work for you. It is important that you have a basic understanding of the principles, so that even if you don't do the work yourself, you have found it worthwhile to read this book.

Beware of promises that sound outrageous. No one can guarantee first-page results on Google for broad searches any longer. Be careful of those who do. And make sure of what they are guaranteeing. It is not hard to get to the first page on Google for "west Toronto one-legged plumbers," but realistically, not many people are searching for that term. Much harder to rank well for "Toronto plumber."

Another point to remember is that most website builders are not marketers. Most of them are not Search Engine Optimization experts, either. Proof of that lies in the terrible condition, SEO-wise, of most websites. A beautiful website is okay if all you want is a brochure. You can then list your web address on your business card and in your advertising. But if you are looking for traffic, you need someone with SEO and marketing knowledge and skills—so when you are getting work done by an outside service provider, use your common sense and ask questions.

Best of luck to you.

APPENDIX 1

Making Movies with Windows Movie Maker
The main point of creating videos is to generate traffic to your website or Google Places listing, so that people learn about your products or service. Of course, an important secondary point is that it helps lift your Places listing above those of your competitors. But to be most effective, it needs to do both.

Early on in this book we talked about the importance of keywords. I am not going to repeat myself here. Suffice it to say that you want the title of your video to contain one or two of your main keywords or keyword phrases. You should have already done the research, so just use your results. Include a location word, such as the name of your town, in the title as well. The nice thing about correct keyword selection for your title is the weight that Google places on videos. Someone searching for your main keyword phrase might wind up seeing your video featured on the first page of results.

You will need a dozen or so photos for a short 60–90 second video. Take pictures of your location, your products, your products in use, or the results of their use. If you already have a website, then maybe you already have graphics available there.

You can name the pictures so that when you import them into Windows Movie Maker they are in the right order. If you use the letters of the alphabet, or numbers before each image name (A Cleaning Product, B Repair Product, C Kitchen Product; or 1 Cleaning Product, 2 Repair Product, 3 Kitchen Product, etc.), they will be in order in Movie Maker after you import them.

So, now you've got your pictures on your computer in a file somewhere, it's time to make a movie. Go to your Start Button and select All Programs, then select Windows Movie Maker (XP) or Windows Movie Maker Live (Windows 7). If you don't have it, for some reason, it's a free download. Google Windows Movie Maker and go to Microsoft's site to get your copy.

I should mention here that Windows Movie Maker, the older version, has some functionality that was removed from Windows Movie Maker Live, the version included on Windows 7. The old version had some audio editing tools and transition timing tools that gave you a little more flexibility. You could get it here http://windows-movie-maker.en.sotonic.com.

There are plenty of sites providing free instruction, including YouTube videos. Just Google "using Windows Movie Maker" and click on the link.
Okay, open Windows Movie Maker and select Add Pictures or Import Pictures, whichever your version of WMM shows you. A window will pop up, and you can

navigate to the folder where you stored your pictures and select them. The thumbnail images will show up on the story board automatically with the latest version of the software, or you may have to select and drag them into place.

You can add an audio track to your movie. There are some nice selections at the website http://incompetech.com/m/c/royalty-free/#

Follow the conditions as outlined on the site under Terms of Use.

You could also try http://www.seabreezecomputers.com/tips/freemusic.htm

Download the audio track you like and then import it into Movie Maker using the Add Audio selection or the Import Audio or Music selection, depending on which version of WMM you have.

Click on Edit Movie or Edit. You will be given some options that allow you to manage the transitions between images. You can also add text to the images. You want to add text to get your message across. You can vary the format of the text and also the position of it in the image.

Once you are satisfied, save your video to your computer, using a file name that includes your main keyword or keyword phrase. Save it in a format for "playback on computer." This will make it YouTube ready. Remember where you saved it to.

Now sign in to YouTube and simply upload your file. While the file is uploading, you can take the time to fill in the title, descriptions, tags, and category—more opportunities for you to use your keywords! The first item in your description should be a link starting with http:// and then your website address. This makes the link live from YouTube. The rest of the description should include details of your location and additional keywords. The tags should include the keywords you want the video to show up for when someone is searching on YouTube. The category should be the closest one to your video's content.

It helps if you can get some folks to watch the video as soon as possible, especially if they give it a good rating. And that's it. Remember, you can't break anything by playing around with software, so go ahead and give it a try. If you don't like your first attempt, junk it and try again. A few hours spent playing with this can have a major impact on traffic to your site and your site's page rank. Keep at it, and good things will happen.

APPENDIX 2

Lifetime Customer Value and Marketing

A critical concept many small business owners never think about, or completely miss the importance of, is the lifetime value of a customer. This concept is critical to your success in business for numerous reasons.

Do you spend money on marketing? Probably. Are you marketing dollars wisely spent? Maybe, maybe not. How do you know? Well, there is an extremely simple way to find out. You can do it in two steps:

1. Find out the lifetime value of an average customer

2. Identify a reasonable marketing cost for attracting that customer

Lifetime Value Calculation

Average Profit (per transaction) x Transactions (per Year) x Years Retained

This is the lifetime value of a customer. Let's make it relatively simple to do. If the average profit per transaction is $10, and the customer makes 6 transactions a year, and we keep that customer for 5 years, their lifetime value to us is $300. This is money in your pocket.

Given the $300 figure, how much should you spend on advertising to acquire a new customer? Well, realistically, anything under $299 leaves you in the black, but making $1 on a $299 investment over 5 years isn't much good. But if you had to spend $100 to get that $300, you are still doing very well. That is a pretty healthy return on your money; better than bank interest, stock market or real estate investments.

You will never know what your return on your marketing investment is if you don't track your marketing efforts and results. To track your results you need to have processes in place to do so and staff educated to collect the information. Charting your gross income every day is a straightforward task. Comparing it to specific marketing efforts requires a little more effort. Having staff asking people what brings them into the store today or asking callers how they learned of your service means they need to be educated about the importance of the question.

Of course, there are more direct ways to identify impact. Marketing that requires people to bring in a coupon, a flyer, or to ask for a specific offer makes it easy to gauge the impact of a particular effort.

Signing up for deals with WagJag, Groupon or Kijiji Daily Deals is easily done, and purchases are tracked through online checkout processes. Of course, you are required to give up a percentage of your sale to the service. The hope is that anyone using these services will return and pay regular price…not always a sure bet.

In any case, knowing your customers lifetime value to you allows you to make smart decisions about marketing. But you will never find that value number unless you are measuring your results accurately.

Jay Abraham tells the story of "Icy Hot", a company that sold a gel that provided relief for arthritis sufferers. Jay asked them what the lifetime value of their customers was. They had no clue. So he sent them away to go and find out. When they came back they had sales numbers that showed their average customer bought from them ten times a year. The jars of Icy Hot sold for three dollars each and cost forty-five cents to make and ship bulk rate. So the value of each customer was about $25 per year.

Knowing this, Jay was able to advise the company to make an offer to radio stations across the country. The offer was the radio stations could keep the revenue from the sale of the product if they advertised it for free. He knew that the first jar of Icy Hot would cost the company a forty-five cent loss, but that each customer would go on to spend another $27.00 with the company for profit per customer of $23.00. that is the power of knowing your customer lifetime value.

Note: The $23.00 profit was only for the first year. Most customers stayed with the company for years. In addition, each package that went out would include coupons and advertising for other products that provided a 20% response rate on the other products. Again, free advertising.

There's another advantage to tracking your customers purchase patterns and frequency. It becomes pretty clear that you can make more money one of three ways, increase the average profit per transaction, increase the number of transactions or increase the retention period. By increasing each component you can have a huge impact on your business. A $12 profit, on 7 transactions a year for 6 years yields a $504 lifetime value, over a 50% increase from the $300 we calculated earlier, but doing that is a topic for a different book.

ABOUT THE AUTHOR

Paul Stevens remembers the days of 1-MB RAM and 40-MB hard drives, the critical specifications of his first computer. He opened his first website in 2003 and worked at it part-time for several years. His interest in using the Internet for local business was piqued when he opened his own bookselling business, and he has been learning and pursuing that interest since 2008.

Paul finally took the plunge to leave his full-time corporate job and now consults with businesses on increasing their Internet traffic, improving their ranking on search engines, and getting more feet through the doors of their establishments.

Paul lives with his wife Lynn, in Hastings, Ontario, the hub of Northumberland Hills internet marketing activity.

To contact Paul about this book, his speaking engagements, or his services, go to:

www.bootstraplocalmarketing.com

Paul Stevens

10831891R00034

Made in the USA
Charleston, SC
08 January 2012